avis

Azrael Aplin

Presentation by *BookLeaf Publishing*

Web: www.bookleafpub.com

E-mail: info@bookleafpub.com

ISBN: 9789357613835

First edition 2022

DEDICATION

nataia calloway

1998-2018

ACKNOWLEDGEMENT

william hurd
tianna jones
kaleigh bloomfield

my hearts, my world, my saviors.
my editors, my critics, my supporters.
thank you.

PREFACE

do you ever wonder...
what it's like to see the world in full color?
to not have the vibrancy dimmed by the looming charcoal despair you're so constantly wrapped in?
to not only feel the warmth of the sun, but be blinded by its aureolin rays of hope that pierce through the cracks between the blacks of your single windows curtain?
to take in the rainbows radiating off the foliage you've nurtured far better than the gardens within you?
to stroll through endless greens and get lost in the beauty nature so desperately wants for you to be encased with?
to love with tenacious reds with no fear of it being spoiled by the maroons you let slip from your olive skin?
oh sweet one, with a shining soul suppressed by shades,
do you ever wonder?

PREFACE

I // perfect

red ribbons flowed from her head-
like a scene of
lusciously intoxicating waterfalls
off a setting sun.

perfectly positioned-
center back.
invisible when facing,
her seemingly cheerful,
olive kissed cheeks.

smiles strewn across her face,
as if they were
permanently placed,
with needle and thread.

and no one saw,
when those fibers were snipped-
and colors fell
greyscale.

for no one ever-
looked back.

II // “love”

all these years
i've been searching for the
"true love"
i’ve been told i was destined
to capture
in this life.
roaming through fields
of withered roses-
letting the thorns pierce through
the thin leather
that be my skin.
sinking to the bottom
of a blackened abyss-
letting the water rush
into the fleshy cavities
of my chest
until there be
no breath.
hiding in the warm comfort
of brut arms
that uplift me in the times of sunlight-
yet subdue me
in the harsh moonlight.
i dance with the devil
on pins of lava

for he hath pursued me
to believe-
hurt
be the only way to get
to the deep dark depths
of the heart.
never once notifying my brain
of the wondrous truth:
that love-
can be painless.

III // fight

i want to be a bird.
to be free from a life
i hadn't chosen.
from the trauma that's left
my body,
mind-
and soul
frozen.
i want to spread my wings-
embrace the sun.
ravish in the calming shot
of lightly freckled flames
and let my fears
run.
i want to chirp from the treetops-
sing a song,
of a life once so
overbearing
and full of
wrong.
and transform it
into the truest battle
i've ever won.

i want to be a bird.

and i mean that-
with every word.

IV // fly

on the ledge of a life that's pushed me
too far to the edge.
contemplating
i've spent my whole life
waiting
for something to make me feel more
than this empty face
searching for stars
in a vacant space.
i'm fading-
ready to drown in the rush of light-
dancing
as my body catches the wind
swirling
the tears of the years
dissipating
and the pounding of my heart stops
pulsating.

V // it's okay

trust yourself enough
to understand:
starting anew
be not a failure,
yet a crucial beginning
to a fresh
and wondrous
journey.

VI // yellow warbler

her tantalizing golden feathers,
captivated my weary eyes-
glistening
within a sky of only pure darkness.

she pulled me in-
instantaneously.
as if her aura,
directly matched her
outward appearance-

and swung away my sorrows,
like they never
even stood
a chance-

i have only touched her
once.
yet she touches me
everyday.

VII // clean

i refuse to feel
any remorse
for your fields
running dry
and soil infertile
when mine is
finally flourishing
after flushing out
the pesticides
brought on
by none other
than your very own
grease stained
fingers.

VIII // peacock

he struts his
iridescent skin
tainted by the ones
he's harmed-
like trophies
growing larger
with every
sparkle he's stolen
and wing
he's bent.

IX // wild goose chase

don't tell me now
that i'm everything
you've wanted.

i've always been
a starling
while you were messing
with the robins.

X // nonconformist

a world without romance-
be a world of
few pleasures
and i for one- refuse
to beseech
such a horror.

XI // icarus

i traced my finger
around the constellations
of your back
interlocking the pattern
of twinkling gravel
that lead to you
becoming
the sun
to me.

XII // eagle

i've had many people
warn me of you-
the extent of your free spirit
and how you may never
succumb
to feelings of love.
yet i ignored them all-
for you have ignited
a fire
within my heart
and soul
that i can't even fathom
living without.
if that means
one day,
i be filled with misery-
i can accept that.
knowing my emotions
be pure-
true,
and irrevocably
for you.

XIII // vulture

no one prepared me for this
i was never cautioned
of a creature
so heinous-
dangerous
so when i was left
tattered and unresponsive

they took a bite.

XIV // …

i feel nothing,
and everything
each moment
every day.

i am an ellipsis
a visual omission

not really existing
but always in the fucking way

XV // relapse

it's as if i can feel the loneliness
seeping through my skin-
agony boiling within my blood,
knocking upon my bones to let it in-
the sorrow keeps collecting in my lungs-
and though i wish to weep,
despair clings to my throat
for a silence it wants to keep.

i've never been pained at the thought
of an empty room.
yet the desire of this abyss, for me: consumed
and i know not what to do,
to rid my existence
of all this gloom.

XVI // seven

their name haunted me -
found its place in all the things i loved,
the streets i wandered,
and songs i sung.
those silly little letters
consistently inserting themselves into my world-
strung up so pretty
like god himself
reveled in my pity.

XVII // raven

the wind rustles my feathers
i am cold
yet unafraid
i am still
yet i move mountains
i am silent
yet screech a thousand melodies

i am a raven-
a contradiction.

dark and mysterious-
light and open.

XVIII // found

there are times in life
where i feel as though
everything is crashing down-
i can’t find any space to breathe
for the air is simply not pristine-
and so silently
i drown.
until i remember,
the tender pressure
of your palm
upon my temple-
how that tiny action
left no room
for a frown to fester
and my mind be filled
with bliss and pleasure
in knowing that
-your hands-
make the struggles of living,
lesser.

XIX // starling

i don't want to be ordinary.
i don't care to be trapped in a routine.

i want to be a reckless bird,
spreading my outrageous wings
and soaring above the cage that is-
normality.

XX // flightless

they placed seed
far above where
my fragile frame
could carry me
and grew
wrath
and resent
when i found
nourishment
upon the ground

XXI // you’re still here

it wasn't until
life had managed
to yank each
tiny fiber
from my body
that i finally
found out
how incredibly strong
one can be
with broken wings

www.ingramcontent.com/pod-product-compliance
Lightning Source LLC
LaVergne TN
LVHW020537160826
845677LV00015B/4120

* 9 7 8 9 3 5 7 6 1 3 8 3 5 *